Crazy Poetry

By Katharine Niffen

Crazy Poetry

By Katharine Niffen

This book is a work of fiction names, characters, business, events, and incidents, are the product of the author's imagination and any resemblance to an actuarial person living or dead or actual events is purely coincidental.

This Book is dedicated to everyone who stood behind me. Who supported me

In following my dreams. For being patient with me in this process

Index

Wild and Dangerous
    Afraid
    If I could
    Be like this
    I'm sorry
    On my knees
    In you
    Got it bad
    The worse day
    Twin Flame
    For you
    Rage
    Got it bad 2
    My way
    Please don't leave
    Lock them up
    Crazy thoughts
    Time
    Calling to me
    Not worthy
    On my knees 2
    Despair
    Everything nice
    What's the point
    Life of the party
    Fighting to survive
    Come with me
    For you 2
    Thump thump thump

Was I thinking
My life
My family
Come and go
My best friend
From you
Don't
Let me fix it
My boy
The thought of you
You
Why
The One
Could You
I see
Going to have you
The Game
Did you Know
Yours
You 2
My Shame
Scared
Sweet Child
The pain
That Word
The Time
The love Recipe
Taken
One of a Kind
Positive
The one 2
Walked In

Unthinkable
Can't Touch
My Girl
Since I met you
What you do
Not going to plead
My obsession
I dream
Love

Wild and Dangerous

Your on my mind
    Twenty four seven
    You're a dangerous thing
    That's going to be
    The death of me
    You're a heartbreaker
    A heart-stopper
    Your wild and crazy
    You're uncontrollable
    Full of fire
    You're everyone's worse nightmare
    Who no one candle handle
    You're going to coast
    Me my freedom
    Living on the wild side
    Making life worth living
    When I'm by your side
    My wild dangerous queen
    You're going to be the death of me

Afraid

Afraid to close my eyes
    To see the light fade away
    To lose the spark
    To fall into darkness
    We're the unknown lives
    And the mystery begins
    Knowing it could be the last time
    Knowing I might not
    Ever see the smile on your face
    To hear your sweet loving voice
    To hug you tight in my arms
    And tell you how much
    I love you
    Knowing I will never
    See you grow old
    Never to be at the kid's weddings
    Are see their baby's being born
    So much I will miss
    All this I know
    All this I keep to myself
    For I know the time is close
    I'm afraid to close my eyes
    To lose what I have
    To lose you and the kids
    To lose all that I love most in life
    My family and friends
    I fear the time is close
    I'm afraid for you and me
    I'm afraid

If I could

I won't change much
    But a couple of things
    I would eat better
    I would take care of myself better
    If I knew what I know now
    Just so I could
    Have more time
    With you in my life
    I never dreamed
    It could be this hard
    That I would meet you so late
    Now it's too late
    Got me wishing for a second chance
    Knowing it's never coming
    For I seen the future
    And I wasn't in it
    Now I living a nightmare
    Knowing I have to leave you behind
    To be with someone else
    To make all your dreams come true
    All because I was a fool

Be like this

I never thought it
    Would be like this
    To be an unknown
    A nobody
    A nothing but a wasted space
    I thought it would be different
    I want to go
    In a blazing glory
    In a heroic act
    A life change moment
    I want to go out on my feet
    Ready to fight to the end
    Not laying on my back
    Like a baby again
    For the time is close
    I have to be ready
    To go out
    Like my ancestors before me
    For it's in my blood
    It's in my bones
    To go out with
    My war paint on

I'm sorry

If you reading this
    It's too late
    I'm sorry
    I didn't make you
    Feel loved by me
    Wanted or important by me
    I did all I could
    To love you
    And to make you happy
    You guys are the most important
    Things in my life
    You guys were all
    I thought about and cared about
    I'm sorry I kept the secret
    But I could not see you all in pain
    I did this for you
    For your happiness
    Meant the world to me
    I could not see you suffer
    As I was dieing so I'm sorry
    But please remember how much
    I love you

On my knees

Down on my knees
    Can't believe it's
    Got to this point
    Never said it would happen
    Can't believe I'm doing it
    Got no choice
    I'm at that point
    There's no turning back
    Wishing it was over
    Ashamed I have to do
    There's nothing else
    Left to do
    So I'm down on my knees
    To pray for my life

In you

I feel the stranger
    In your embrace
    Hear it in your voice
    See it in your eyes
    I feel the danger
    In your place
    You give me no choice
    Got me thinking twice
    Fearing for my life
    For evil lives
    Inside you
    Don't want to pay
    The price
    I just want to survive
    Live a long life
    For this is true
    Don't want to be
    Someone's sacrifice

Got it bad

Always on my mind
Twenty four-seven
Seeing you everywhere
Talking about you
All the time
People say I'm obsessed
When it comes to you
Your in my dreams
In my nightmares
There's no escaping
I'm losing my mind
I can't eat
Without winding about you
Thinking of your embrace
Our first kiss
The magical nights with you
Blows my mind
You're my heart's desire
Got me living in a fantasy world
Trying to keep it together
But it's hopeless
When it comes to you
You're my fantasy girl
My other half
My dream lover
My soulmate

The Worse day

The worse day
Every parent fears
But can't be stoped
Is the very first day of school
Of the child's life
Yes preschool
For they know
The nightmare will begin
They send a loving
Peaceful happy child
No one can explain it
No one knows how it happens
But from that first day on
The parents
Will never know peace
Or quit or rest again
For their sweet child
Has returned different
To cause destruction
And be disobedient
To drive their parents insane
For their sweet child
Has been transformed
Into an unstoppable monster of destruction

For you

You're my heart and soul
My twin flame
Born to be one
My vow to you
I will make
True for eternity
My love will grow stronger
My flame will burn brighter
For you
For I will love no other
Want no other
Think of no other
For my great belongs to you
I will do everything in my power
To make you happy
For we are one
Creating the ultimate love
That will grow
That will burn for eternity
For you are my heart and soul
My twin flame

For you

I stood by you
Day after day
Watching you love another
Pouring out your heart and soul
Watching your love grow
As time went on
Never letting you know
The way I felt
Was my mistake
Watching you take your vows
In holy matrimony
With a smile on my face
Broke my heart into a million pieces
Seeing how much you adore another
As our friendship grew
It tore me apart
Knowing your being loved by another
In the perfect way
Brings peace to my soul
As I stand by your side year after year
As your family grows
My love grows stronger
For knowing I did right by you

Rage

I've seen the rage
    The uncontrollable temper
    Keeps me nervous
    Knowing its coming
    Won't be able to stop it
    Now it's too late
    All tied up
    No way to move
    Scared to make a sound
    Terrified to make him mad
    Fearing for my life
    Knowing theirs no escape
    As the fist come flying
    Blood starts flowing
    Pleading for my life
    As I lose consciousness
    Breathing by a machine
    Praying to survive
    For I seen the rage

Got it bad

I need you
    I can't take
    Your denial
    Need you by my side
    To hold you tight
    Kiss you long
    Love you all night
    Please don't say no
    Don't take the magic away
    Needing you
    More than ever
    To light up my world
    Set my heart on fire
    For I got it bad
    Calling out your name
    Screaming for your touch
    Aching for your love
    Please don't say no
    Don't break my heart
    Don't kill my soul
    Don't destroy our love
    For I got it bad

My way

It's my way
    Or no way
    Love me all night
    Love me right
    Hold me tight
    Kiss me long
    Give me sweet talk
    Seduce me
    Make me yours
    Call out my name
    Make me weak
    At my knees
    Be my lover
    Be my friend
    Be my spouse
    Do it right
    Do it now
    Do it for us

Please don't leave

My life my world
   Is in chaos
   Turned upside down
   Don't know
   How I will make it through
   I can't lose you
   Can't lose my love
   I can't survive
   Without you by my side
   Please don't leave me
   Please don't leave
   It will kill me
   If you were not here
   If I could not see you
   If I could not hear your voice
   If I could not love you
   Please don't destroy me
   Please don't destroy our love
   Please don't kill my soul
   I need you
   I love you
   More than ever
   So please don't leave me
   Please don't leave me

Lock them up

Lock up the boys tonight
    The girls are out on the prowl
    Going to get their man

      Nothing going to stop them
      When they're on the hunt
      Lock the boys up
      Got to protect them
      From the wild bunch
      Out on the hunt
      Throw away the key
      To keep them safe
      From the crazy ones
      Lock up the boys
      The girls got the hunger
      They're looking for your sons
      The good boys the bad boys
      They want them all
      Daddy can't protect them
      The girls won't quit
      Until they get your boys
      Got to lock up the boys
      Got to keep them safe
      For the girls are out on the prowl
      Looking for your boys
      Going to get their man

Crazy thoughts

I set here all alone
      Can't get the thoughts out of my head
      Knowing I'm disposable
      That I ant nothing special to anyone
      My heart beats a mile a minute
      My mind going crazy
      Should I do it or should I not
      Is the question that runs through my head
      Wounding if anyone would care or give a dam
      Would they even know I'm gone
      It's all insane I know
      Knowing it's all a lie
      Wounding why my mind treats me this way
      My heart feels one way and my mind goes another
      Am I going insane
      Wounding if everyone is going through this
      Trying to hold my head up high
      Doing all I can to fight these insane thoughts
      Laying in a hospital bed wounding where it all went wrong
      Wearing my heart on my sleeve
      Fighting for my life living on a machine
      Can't open my eyes or say a word
      Hoping you're there praying for me
      Can't believe I was so stupid
      To do this to everyone what was I thinking
      To destroy everyone I know ripping apart their heart
      Demolishing their soul Because I was a fool
      When I tried to take my life
      Believing I didn't have your love
      I was blind to see what was before me

Now I pray that you will forgive me
And keep on loving me
As much as I love you

Time

Time has come
    Time has past
    Saying the same
    As it always has
    Repeating what has been done before
    To happen again
    In time not yet here
    Going through the emotions
    Like ancestors before us
    And a generation yet to come
    Love and hate war and peace
    Time tells it all
    If you only pay attention
    You will see
    What time has to say
    For time has come
    Time has past
    Did you pay attention
    To what time
    Had to say

Calling to me

I hear your name

In a whispers calling
Out to me
As your beauty
Shines the way
To the greatest
Treasure there is
Created by
All the god's magic
Into the rarest gem
I feel your pull

Reaching out to me
As the angels sing
Of your glory
I hear you calling
For me
In the winds
As they blow-by
I hear you
Calling me

Not Worthy

I knew it
When I first saw you
There was something about you
That drives me insane
Your beauty, your caring soul
Your loving heart
That lights up my world
A miracle from heaven
Who stole my heart
Knowing it's crazy
Knowing I'm not worthy
Of your love of your greatness
Not worthy
To be in your presence
Or in your life
Not worthy
To even know your name
I'm not worthy
To love you
Or to know you

On my knees 2

Down on my knees
Kissing the ground
You walk upon
Begging for your mercy
Pleading for forgiveness
Knowing I did you wrong
Hurting you in the way I did
Breaking your heart
Crushing your soul
Being disloyal
Losing your trust
Losing your faith in me
Because I was a fool
Taking you for granted
Believing you will always be there
Was a sign of my stupidity
Praying you still
Love me
Down on my knees
Begging like no
To give me one more chance
To love you
The way I should
The way you were meant to be loved
Like a queen

Despair

I live in the
Shadows of despair
Never to see
The light of love
For my crimes
Of passion
Against humanity
Never learning my lesson
Thought I was better
Then all the rest
Now I'm sinking
Lower than ever
Deep down in despair
No way out
Until I'm forgiven
From those, I crushed
In my little games
Who cursed me
Out of pain
To suffer in despair

Everything nice

Give me a little
   Bit of sugar
   Give me a little
   Bit of spice
   And we will make
   Everything nice
   A little bit of honey
   A tab bit of chocolate
   Ooh ain't that sweet
   Blow a kiss

   Whisper something nice

   Oh it's getting steamy
   Stir it once
   Stir it twice
   To make it extra nice
   Give me something sweet
   A little bit scealent
   Give a little love
   There's no stopping us now
   Got it hot in here

What's the point

I can't understand it

Am I that bad
  Why do they all hate me

  Why don't they

Don't want me around

  Won't even talk to me
  What did I do wrong
  Why do they all leave me
  How come no one loves me
  Am I a waste
  Am I worthless
  Should I make everyone happy
  And just put
  An end to it all
  Since my love
  Isn't enough for anyone
  What's the point
  For me to carry on
  Since I don't matter
  To anyone anymore
  What's the point

Life of the party

I got it going on
There's no stopping me
Can't get enough of me
I bring the laughs
I bring the tricks
For I got it all
I'm the life of the party
Center of attention
Everywhere I go
Making everyone feel better
I'm the one everyone loves
To be around
Putting smiles on everyone's faces
Bring cheer to them all
The one they all look up to
For I'm the one who
Put's love in their hearts
For I'm the life of the party

Fighting to survive

I had it all
In a blink of an eye
I lost it all
Nothing but the clothes
On my nack
To keep me warm
Sleeping on the streets
Got no roof over my head
No where to turn
No were to go
Things got bad
Real quick for us all
Everyone's fighting to keep
A roof over their head
And food to eat
Trying to stay warm
In the middle of winter
Shoes got holes in the soles
Fighting to survive
The hard streets
Fighting to get
Back what I lost
A roof to stay under
And food to eat
The things I took for granted
Never realizing
How lucky I was
Now I'm fighting to survive

Come with me

Come with me
To run through
The grass barefoot
To have a little fun
Come with me
To the beach
To feel the sand between our toes
As the waves
Hit the shores
To have some fun
Come with me on a hike
Through the woods
To see nature at its best
To have a blast
Come with me
To have the best
Time of your life
To hangout
With your best friend
To be with me

For you 2

I will fight a lion
I will fight a tiger
Evan a panter
All for you
I will wonder in the outback
I will wonder
In the African jungle
All for you
I will fight the beast
That lives in the night
I will fight
The great white shark
All for you
I will wonder
On Mount Everest
All for you
For your love
Is worth it all

Thump thump thump

One can lead into two
Two can lead into four
Most don't even
Think about it
But knows it happens
Day in and day out
Keeps us going
Without skipping a beat
Thump thump thump
It goes
It's a beat of life
Can't live without it
One beats leads
Into two beats
It's the perfect rhythm
Of life
The one and only
Heart Beat

What was I thinking

I don't know about you
But I'm going crazy
Got no tv
Got no phone
Got no entertainment
Go me going insane
Got no food
Got no drinks
Got no shelter
What was I thinking
This surviving crap
In the jungle
Blows my mind
I must be insane
To leave my home
All the comforts of life
To play in the jungle

My Life

I see my life pass me by
    The good times I had
    With my friends and family
    The ups and downs
    We all shared together
    That made us laugh and cry
    The pain I feel
    As I am passing away
    The heartbreak I'm going through
    Is the worse of it all
    For I know
    I'm cousin them more pain
    I will ever go through
    My life has been great
    That I can not deny
    For the love of my family and friends
    Make me rich
    As I pass away
    I hope they don't cry or mourn over me
    For they made my life worth living

My Family

I love them all
   They come to be

      In different ways
      Some by blood
      Others by choice
      Others by marriage
      All have different names
      Mother, Father, Son, and Daughter
      In-laws of all kinds
      Don't forget them
      Special grandbabies, special friends
      That comes into your life
      All their kids who I love
      Like my own
      All become my family
      Don't want to lose
      Anyone of them
      For I will go insane
      They're my heart and soul
      Who I can't live without
      They're all I call my family

Come and go

We come and we go
    But what we do in-between
    Who we love
    Share are hearts with
    Makes all the difference
    In the world
    We can go as nothing
    Or we can live for eternity
    Depending on how
    We live our lives
    We can make
    It wild and memorable
    Or vanish into nothing
    All depending
    On who you leave behind
    But we all
    Come and go
    Choose the way
    You want it to be

My Bestfriend

Are special and unique
A little bit wild
A little bit crazy
A little bit insane
Their caring and loving
Supportive and butt-kicking
A little bit adventures
A little bit compassionate
A little bit outgoing
Their one of a kind
That's for sure
A little bit hot-headed
But I wouldn't
Have it any other way
They're the best
They're my best friend

From you

A bullet a knife
A tiger a lion
A tank an aircraft bomber
The army
The marines
Not even the navy
Are the USA air force
Could keep me from you
No prison built
Could stop me
No ocean wide enough
To stop me
Nothing in the world
Or in the universe
Could stop me
From getting to you
For you are mine

Don't

Don't look don't think
    Don't touch don't talk
    To what is mine
    She's off-limits
    To everyone but me
    She's mine
    Will always be mine
    And nobody else's
    Don't make the mistake
    Don't piss me off
    You don't want
    To become a waste
    For she is mine
    So don't be stupid
    With what is mine
    Just don't
    With mine

Let me fix it

I got what it takes
　　To fix what is broken
　　Don't worry
　　I don't just use duck tape
　　I got the perfect grip
　　To hold it right
　　I grease it up
　　To fit it tight
　　It's a guarantee
　　I mend I fix
　　What is broken
　　Put the pieces together
　　To last forever
　　To give satisfaction
　　Is what I do best
　　When I'm done
　　You will know
　　You've been healed
　　You've been loved
　　The perfect way

My Boy

My boy my precious son
    My one and only
    Who has half my heart
    Who taught me to love
    Who taught me patience
    Who made me cry
    And brought me laughter
    Sometimes I want to kill him
    Sometimes I want to hug him
    But I would not trade him
    For anything in the world
    He's my sweet loving boy
    Sometimes a pain in my ass
    Sometimes my pride and joy
    He's a handful
    He's full of surprises
    He's a poet
    He's an Author
    A creator at heart
    He's my precious son

The thought of you

The thought of you
    Drives my soul
    It's the reason
    My heart beats
    It controls every
    Move I make
    You're the reason
    I wake up in the morning
    The reason I cry in the night
    For the thought of you
    Drives my passion
    For you are the reason
    I will be on bended knee
    The thought of you
    Who holds the key
    To my future
    The thought of loving you
    For the rest of my life
    Drives my desire
    The thought of you
    Being mine

You

Your touch
>Gives me strength
>Your smile
>Gives me courage
>Your kiss
>Gives me life
>Without you
>I could not exist
>Your eyes
>Light up my life
>Your smile
>Feels me with joy
>Your touch
>Drives my passion
>Without you
>I'm worthless
>You are my heart
>You are my soul
>You are my compassion
>You're my world
>You're my life
>You're my love

Why

Why do you
> Do this to me
> Is it fun for you
> To see me in pain
> Does it warm your heart
> To break mine
> Does it make you laugh
> When you got me crying
> Does it make you feel better
> When you put me through hell
> Why do you do this to me
> When you know
> I will do anything for you
> When I give you
> My heart and soul
> Why can't you
> Let me love you
> The way you're meant
> To be loved
> To hold you
> And never let you go
> To break down
> The wall you built
> To fix your broken heart
> Why can't you see
> I'm not going anywhere
> I'm here for eternity
> You won't chase me away
> Why why why

Can't you see
I love you

The One

I want to be the one
    You dream of
    The one who brings
    Your joy and happiness
    The one who puts
    The smile on your face
    The one you hold
    Tight in your arms
    I want to be
    The one you wake up to
    The one who fills
    All your fantasy
    The one you cry for
    Who your scared to lose
    The one who's by your side
    In the future to come
    The one who makes
    You forget your past
    I want to be the one you love
    The one you're married to

Could you

Could you be the one
    To hold me tight
    To kiss me long
    To win my heart
    To show me, true love
    Could I be the one
    To romance you every night
    To take your breath away
    When I kiss you
    To tame the wild beast
    When I love you
    To take you to heaven
    When I hold you tight
    Could you be the one
    That I will hold
    That I will kiss
    That I will love
    For eternity
    Could I be the one
    That captures your heart
    That captures your love
    To be your's forever

I see

I see you
>Looking at my queen
>I know what your thinking
>You better change your mind
>For she's taking
>This is your last warning
>Don't talk don't look
>At my beauty queen
>I see you sneaking
>Around behind my back
>Doing all you can
>To be by my queen
>Trying to take my place
>At my queen's side
>Don't take me a fool
>I see what you're doing
>This is your last chance
>To leave her alone
>For she's my beautiful queen
>My sweet loving queen
>So take your leave
>Or pay the price
>Which is guarantee
>I see what you're doing
>So take my warning
>Or pay the price

Going to have you

You're the finest
    Your the prettiest
    I ever seen
    A rare gem indeed
    Who's got me heated
    Oh yeah you're going to be mine
    For I have the best
    And you are
    Finer than the rares diamond
    Hotter than a Rubie
    You're going to make
    Me greate
    Oh yeah going to be mine
    For I can't have it any other way
    For I have the best
    You will put it all to shame
    You're too sexy to handle
    Too valuable to hideaway
    You're a treasure to all
    Oh yeah you're going to be mine
    There's no doubt about it
    Going to be mine

The Game

I'm a player
>I'm a gambler
>In the game of life
>In the game of love
>Looking for the big win
>Playing what I'm dealt
>Taking every chance
>No bet too small
>No bet too large
>Playing to win
>Can't afford to lose
>The chips are stacked
>Up against me
>But I won't quit until I win
>For the game is calling me
>Got to hit it hard
>Calling the bluff
>Looking for a flush
>To win it all
>To win the game
>To win in life

Did you know

I'm in pain
That I cry every time I'm alone
My heart is broken
My soul is crushed
Can't control my emotions
All because of you
I poured out my soul
Opened up my heart
Fell deeply in love
Did you know
You're the only one
I ever loved
I waited a lifetime for you
Turning down everyone
That wanted me
Just to be with you
Did you know
That I'm lost
That I'm suffering
I cry myself to sleep
Thinking about you
Wondering why I'm not good enough
Not good enough for your love
Not good enough to be with you
Did you know
You have my heart and soul
You hold my future
My dreams in your hands
You hold my love
Did you know

You hold my life in your hands
Did you know

Your's

You take my breath away
I lose all control
I can't stop this feeling
I have for you
I'm burning up
With desire
You set me on fire
Got me under your spell
Hooked me right from the start
With hazel eyes
And that beautiful smile
I'm putty in your hands
Your's to control
Had me loving you
From the start

You 2

My heart and soul
Is a part of you
My dreams and desires
Are all because of you
My life
Is all about you
For I live
To make you happy
To please you
To cherish you
To love you
It's all about you
Will always be
All about you

My Shame

I was young and innocent
Not knowing the evil
In this world
I was trusting and loving
Of the ones
Who were to protect me
Not knowing the monster
Within them
Not knowing the changs
I was going through
As my childhood was being stolen
Bit by bit my fear grew
Because the ones I love
Not knowing who to trust
As my innocents
Was being stolen in the night
Scared to cry scared to tell
Afraid to anger the monster
In my house
The scar's on the inside
Can't compare to the ones on the outside
Hiding the shame
Keeping the secret
As I grew
As it continues to destroy me
For no justice will ever come
That can restore my innocents and childhood

Scared

Living in the dark
    Hungry and cold
    It hurts inside and out
    Scared most of the time
    Can't understand what's going on
    Loving and caring one moment
    Angry and terrifying the next
    Living in fear
    Turning black and blue
    From the monster inside of you
    Crying for mercy
    Begging for your love
    Only to get your anger
    Don't know what I did
    To get your hate
    Hope it's not too late
    I still love you
    And scared to be around you
    Living in fear
    Because of you

Sweet Child

Born out of love
　　That turned into hate
　　Battered and bruised
　　Tormented and tortured
　　Every waking moment
　　A precious child
　　Fighting for survival
　　Laying in a hospital
　　On life support
　　Dreaming of being loved
　　Cherished and protected
　　From the beast
　　Called family
　　Who abused
　　In an angry rage
　　A sweet loving child
　　Now fighting to live
　　Who was loved now hated
　　The damage is done
　　It will not be forgotten
　　The scars run deep
　　But this loving child
　　Is a survivor

The Pain

It's too late
    To love you
    For the damage is done
    I've been destroyed
    Being with you
    Is like a chore I hate
    Done with no feelings
    Done with no passion
    Done with no love
    The wall is built
    To protect what's left
    Believing your all the same
    Just want to use and mistreat
    Like a piece of trash
    Can't trust anyone
    Can't believe the lies
    You all tell
    For it's all the same
    Nothing but tricks
    To get your way
    No more love to give
    Can't handle the pain

That Word

Don't know how to
Don't know if I can
Don't really want to
Say that word
It breaks my heart
It hurts my soul
To know I don't have a choice
To say what will destroy me
For I still love you
I still need you
I still think about you
I can't do it
I can't let you go
Please don't make
Me say the word
Knowing it won't be over
When I say it
For I still love you
Can't take the pain
Can't handle the suffering
Can't let you go
Can't say that

The Time

The time is close
    I feel it coming
    Praying it won't happen
    Not ready to go
    Still got lots to do
    Hoping I won't be forgotten
    By the ones I love
    Prayin I brought love
    And joy to their lives
    Praying they won't hurt long
    After I'm gone
    Hoping they will remember
    All the good times we had
    Praying to see them again
    On the other side
    Praying I see heaven
    And not hell
    When I cross over

The Love Recipe

A dash of sweetness
A lot of kindness
A lot of passion
A wink here and there
A few smiles
A dash of humor
A splash of mystery
A sprinkle of badness
All the right words
Will get you
A lot of hugs
A lot of kisses
A lot of love

Taken

I'm broken
Cried for years
Hated everyone
Didn't trust anyone
I'm lost
Missing a part of me
Trying to live
With a hole in my heart
Only memories to turn to
So I won't forget
The way it was
The laughter
The joy and love
I use to have
Your voice
Your face
Your love
I'm a scared to lose
As it fades away from me
Since the day
You were taken from me

One of a kind

My bady is one of a kind
>That's the way I like it
>My bady loves country music
>Horror films
>Good old home cooking
>And ice-cold pop
>Sleeping in late
>Playing with the kids
>My baby loves back rubs
>Holding hands
>Kissing long
>Holding me tight
>Cuddling all night
>My baby loves surprises
>Writing poetry
>Hanging out with the family
>My baby Loves
>Being with me
>Loving me right

Positive

I got all the symptoms
   That I can not lie
   I've been tested
   And it came back
   Positive
   I can't believe it
   I took all the precautions
   I was told to take
   And I still caught it
   Don't know what to do
   Or how to get rid of it
   Can't believe I was exposed
   No medicine can help
   That's it's too late
   Their nothing anyone can do
   For I've been struck by love

The One 2

You got me going crazy
    My dream girl
    My fantasy girl
    Seeing you everywhere
    Got me on my toes
    Got me chasing after you
    Like it's a game
    But I won't stop
    For your my one and only
    My dream girl
    My fantasy girl
    The one that drives me crazy
    But I can't stop
    Chasing you
    You're my supermodel
    My beauty queen
    Got my head spinning
    You're my future
    My destiny
    The one I got to have
    So let the games begin
    For I won't stop
    You're my supermodel
    My beauty queen
    My one and only
    Who drives me crazy
    I won't stop
    I won't lose
    You're my dream girl
    My fantasy girl

The one I'm crazy about

Walked In

It's getting hot in here
I'm getting heated
When you walked into the room
You got my blood a boiling
My temperature a rising
That I can't deny
Got me sweating
Got me nervous
It's getting hard to talk
Since you came into the room
I don't know what it is
That go me going crazy
I don't understand it
Got my heart beating faster
I might have a heart attack
Got my staring
Got me acting a fool
Since you came into the room
I can't help myself
I can't control it
I can't stop it
It's driving me crazy
Got me acting like a kid again
Can't stop smiling
Got me losing it
Since you walked into the room

Unthinkable

This is not about my dog
This is not about my truck
It's about a special love
No matter the coast
Setting in a dark room all alone
For doing the unthinkable
Never thought it possible
Know there was no other choice
Standing up for what's right
Refusing to be a victim
While being terrified
As the fear grew stronger
Knowing it's now or never
Doing what is right
To save a life
Got me serving life
Got to survive
Took the chance
Got no regrets
For I did the unthinkable

Can't Touch

You're the most beautiful
    I ever seen
    I'm burning up inside
    I'm going insane
    You're an angel from above
    Perfect in every way
    You got me heated
    You're sexy as hell
    But I can't touch
    For you'll off limits
    You belong to another
    And it's killing me inside
    Got me dreaming
    Of a fantasy world
    Where were together
    My beautiful queen
    You'll a perfect ten
    Who's got me going crazy
    Always running through my mind
    Who touched my heart
    But I can't touch
    For you'll off limits
    You belong to another
    And it's killing me inside
    I've fallen head over heel
    Deeply in love
    Now there's no turning back
    You stole my heart
    Dreaming to be with you
    But I can't touch

My Girl

Started out with a pic
Made me take a double look
A text here and there
Got me excited
Got me hooked
At first sight
Now I can't leave
For I'm in love
Now we never be apart
I can't believe
It started with a pic
That took my breath away
Had me hooked
At first sight
What a great life
Spending my nights and days
With you
It was magic
When I got a sight
Of the pic
That began my life
With you
Can't believe it began with a pic

Since I met you

Oh what a fool I've been
    Looking in all the wrong places
    Until I met you
    Oh how my life
    Got turned upside down
    Now I'm confused
    Lost in this time and space
    Thought I had it all
    Until I met you
    Now my head a spinning
    My heart a racing
    Don't know what to do
    Got me confessing
    All my dirty little emotions
    Spilling all my wild fantasies
    I must be going crazy
    Believe I had it all
    Until I met you
    I'm not the same
    For you changed me
    Got me dreaming
    Of the future
    By your side
    Since I met you

What you do

I see wha you're doing
    Saying it's in your nature
    But I can't believe it
    Saying it's just a game
    That you can't be changed
    It's a thing we all do
    Having a little fun
    Every chance you get
    Got me thinking
    Got me praying
    I'm not the next one
    It's more than
    A little fun for me
    I've been warned
    But I'm taking the chance
    That I'm not like the rest
    That you play your games on
    I see what you're doing
    Saying it's in your nature
    It's just what you do
    Hoping I'm not the next one
    You do this to

Not going to plead

I'm not going to beg
    I'm not going to plead
    For I'm better than that
    I'm one of a kind
    A special breed
    A little bit wild
    A little bit crazy
    But I ant not fool
    I know what you're doing
    You Can't hide it from me
    You're not going to break my heart
    You're not going to crush my soul
    No need to sneak around
    The doors are wide open
    I'll be fine
    I don't need your lies
    I don't need your pity
    I don't need your game
    For I'm bigger than that
    It's no sweat off my back
    I'll be better off
    After I kick you out the door
    I'm not going to beg
    I'm not going to plead
    Or waste my time
    Over trash like you

My Obsession

I've got an obsession
    Like no other
    It's not overeating
    It's not drinking
    It's not even playing the cards
    For they don't compare
    To my obsession
    I can't stop thinking about
    My obsession
    Takes up all my time
    There's nothing else
    That drives me crazy
    Some say I need help
    But I think I'm fine
    With my obsession
    Don't want no one around
    Don't want no one thinking about
    My obsession
    I might be insane
    But I can't control it
    I don't understand it
    Why I'm so possessive
    Over my obsession

I Dream

I dream of paradise
    I dream of heaven
    But they don't exist
    Without you by my side
    I can't stop dreaming of you
    How wonderful it would be
    If we were stranded
    On a deserted Ialasnd
    We're I can have you
    All by myself
    Laying on the beach
    Drinking coconut water
    Oh I can't stop thinking
    Of you and me together
    Raising a family
    Growing old
    Taking on the world
    Side by side
    You and me baby
    To the end
    How great it would be
    I can't stop dreaming
    Of you and me

Love

L is for lust
    I have for you
    O is for my obsession
    Of you
    V is fr how vulnerable
    You make me feel
    E is for eternity
    Which I want to spend with you
    For love is wild
    Makes you do crazy things
    Gets you to lose your insanity
    Makes you act like a fool
    For the special one
    L is for lecherous feeling
    I have for you
    O is for my one and only
    Heart's desire
    V is for my venust
    Queen
    E is for ecstasy
    That you got me feeling
    For love means so much
    It would take a lifetime
    To explain
    All the ways
    I love you

A little bit about Katharine Niffen. She is an aspiring author, she has a great deal of passion for writing. She enjoys making people smile with her writing. Besides being a living grandma. She's a caring daughter and mother. Dedicated to pursuing her dreams.